# BARNABAS

## THE ENCOURAGER

**TOLD BY CARINE MACKENZIE**
**ILLUSTRATIONS BY FRED APPS**

Copyright © 2007 Carine Mackenzie
Published by Christian Focus Publications, Geanies House,
Fearn, Tain, Ross-shire, IV20 1TW, Scotland, U.K.
Printed in China.
ISBN: 978-1-84550-290-4
www.christianfocus.com

**CF4·K**
Because you're never
too young to know Jesus

Barnabas came from the island of Cyprus in the Mediterranean Sea. His family belonged to the tribe of Levi, who were the priests for the Jewish people.

Barnabas became a follower of the Lord Jesus Christ. His name as a child was Joses but the church leaders gave him the name Barnabas, which means Son of Encouragement, because of his attitude to and treatment of other believers in the Lord.

The people in the early church in Jerusalem were united in love with each other. They shared all their possessions. Some sold their land and houses and gave the money for use by all the believers as they needed.

Barnabas sold some land that he owned. He brought the money to the church leaders. They would use it for the needs of the church people.

Barnabas showed sympathetic concern for the fellow-believers, not just by words but by his actions.

The church faced great difficulties. Many people were persecuted for their faith in Jesus. Some were even put to death.

Saul was one of those who hated the Lord's people. He went on a special journey to Damascus to arrest believers.

But God had other plans. Saul had a miraculous meeting with the Lord on the road to Damascus. His life was turned around. He was now one of the believers too.

Instead of harming the followers of Jesus, Saul was preaching the gospel in the synagogues.

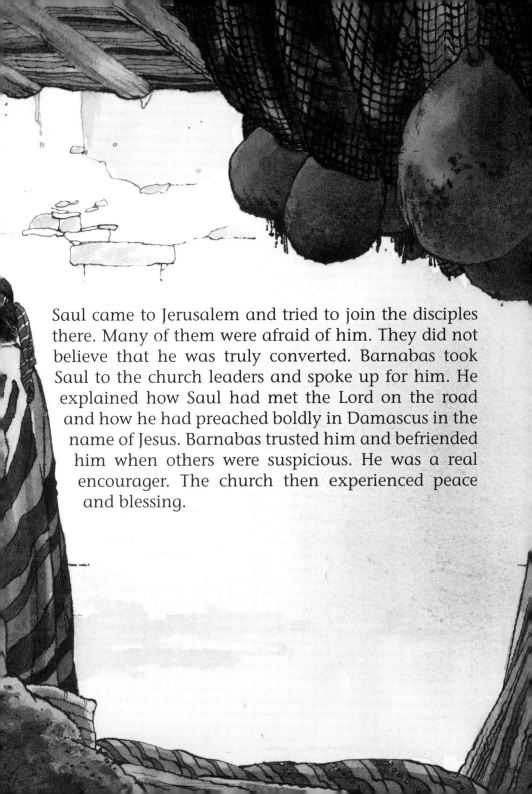

Saul came to Jerusalem and tried to join the disciples there. Many of them were afraid of him. They did not believe that he was truly converted. Barnabas took Saul to the church leaders and spoke up for him. He explained how Saul had met the Lord on the road and how he had preached boldly in Damascus in the name of Jesus. Barnabas trusted him and befriended him when others were suspicious. He was a real encourager. The church then experienced peace and blessing.

When the church was being persecuted, many believers fled from Jerusalem. Some settled in Antioch, about three hundred miles north of Jerusalem. At first they preached the gospel of Jesus only to the Jews but later preached the Lord Jesus to the Greeks. God blessed them and many were converted.

When news of this reached Jerusalem, the church leaders decided to send Barnabas to encourage them.

Barnabas was so glad to see the grace of God at work in their lives. He encouraged them to continue with the Lord. Barnabas was a good man, full of faith and the Holy Spirit. He trusted in the Lord Jesus Christ and obeyed God's word.

Many people were added to the church there as a result of Barnabas' work.

Barnabas went to Tarsus to find his friend Saul. He wanted his help in the church at Antioch. What an encouragement that would have been to Saul.

For a whole year Barnabas and Saul taught and preached in the church at Antioch. Believers were given the name "Christians" first in Antioch.

Barnabas and Saul were given the task of taking relief aid to the needy believers in Judea. Word had been brought to Antioch warning of a great famine that was due. So the church people there gave what they could to help, and sent it to the church in Judea.

Barnabas and Saul were trustworthy and hard-working. They returned to Antioch after delivering the famine relief and took with them John Mark, a cousin of Barnabas. Barnabas and Saul were among the leaders in the Antioch church.

God the Holy Spirit gave the instruction, "Separate Barnabas and Saul for my special work."

So the other church leaders, after prayer and fasting, laid hands on them and sent them out on a missionary journey. John Mark went too as their assistant.

The first stop on their preaching tour was the island of Cyprus, where Barnabas had been brought up. They then sailed to Perga in Asia Minor.

John Mark decided to leave the group and returned to Jerusalem. But Barnabas and Paul (Saul's Greek name) continued to preach the word of God boldly. Some Jews opposed their teaching, but many Gentiles (non-Jews) believed.

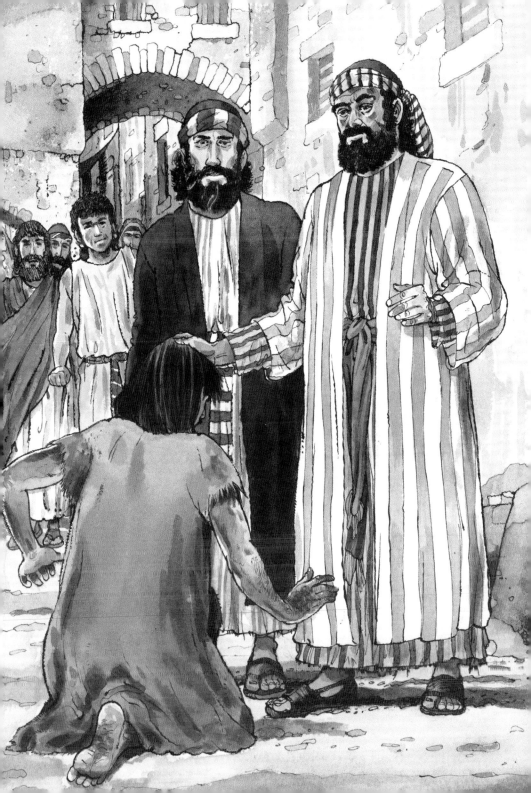

Paul and Barnabas explained that God's word had come first to the Jews, but they had rejected it. God had commanded them to bring the good news to the Gentiles. They were glad to hear it. The word of the Lord spread all through the region.

Barnabas and Paul suffered persecution for preaching God's word. They were expelled from the area so they travelled on to Lystra. A lame man there heard Paul speaking. Paul realised he had faith to be healed. "Stand up straight on your feet," he ordered. The man leapt up and walked.

The people were amazed at what had happened. "The gods have come down to us," they shouted. A pagan priest came out with oxen and garlands to lead worship to the two men they thought were gods.

But Barnabas and Paul were distressed. They tore their clothes and cried out. "We are men just like you. Do not worship us. The living God, who made heaven and earth and all things, is the one you should worship."

The mood of the crowd soon changed. The same people who wanted to worship Barnabas and Paul, soon started to throw stones in hatred.

They dragged Paul out of the city, leaving him for dead. He recovered however and went back into the city. The next day he and Barnabas left.

False teachers started to teach wrong doctrine. Barnabas and Paul disputed with them and eventually decided to take the matter to the church leaders in Jerusalem. Peter spoke up declaring that salvation comes only through the grace of the Lord Jesus Christ.

Barnabas and Paul told the company how many miracles and wonders God had worked through them among the Gentile people.

Agreement was reached. Barnabas and Paul returned to work in Antioch teaching and preaching the word with many other helpers.

"Let's go back and visit all the places we went to on our first missionary journey," Paul said to Barnabas. "We will see how they are doing."

Barnabas agreed but was determined to take John Mark with them again. Paul was not willing to do that. He remembered how John Mark had left them at Perga and not continued with the work.

The disagreement was so sharp that Paul and Barnabas decided to part company. Paul chose Silas as his travelling companion for the next missionary journey.

Barnabas wanted to give John Mark another chance and he took him to Cyprus.

In later years Paul admitted that John Mark was a useful worker and helped in his ministry. Barnabas had encouraged him in the work.

Barnabas the encourager was a great man of God.

He preached boldly. He showed great love and concern for fellow-believers, encouraging many to continue in the grace of God.

His main message was that Jesus Christ is the only way to be saved, both for Jew and Gentile.

You too must believe this message and pass it on to others.